How to Find Love

How to
Find Love

Published in 2017 by The School of Life
First published in the USA in 2018
70 Marchmont Street, London WC1N 1AB
Copyright © The School of Life 2017
Designed and typeset by Marcia Mihotich
Printed in Latvia by Livonia Print

A proportion of this book has appeared online at
www.theschooloflife.com/thebookoflife

Every effort has been made to contact the copyright holders of
the material reproduced in this book. If any have been
inadvertently overlooked, the publisher will be pleased to make
restitution at the earliest opportunity.

The School of Life is a resource for helping us understand
ourselves, for improving our relationships, our careers and our
social lives – as well as for helping us find calm and get more
out of our leisure hours. We do this through creating films,
workshops, books and gifts.

www.theschooloflife.com

ISBN 978-0-9955736-9-7

10 9 8 7 6 5

Contents

I
Introduction:
From Reason
to Instinct

We should feel sympathy for ourselves. The challenges of finding love are highly complex, seldom systematically explored, and relatively new. We have been looking for love the way we do now for, at best, only 260 years. We are still at the dawn of determining how to get into good relationships. Signs of our missteps are all around us.

For most of history, relationships were very different in two main ways. Firstly, people didn't marry for love. They did so for reasons of status, money, household skills and beauty. We didn't expect to *love* our partners; we hoped – at best – to tolerate them. We made Marriages of Reason. Secondly, we didn't have to find our partners ourselves. The task of locating a spouse was left to our families or society more broadly. We would wait to be presented with options vetted for us according to 'objective' criteria.

Then, in the middle of the 18th century in Europe, a revolution of ideas began that has now spread around the world; a movement known to us today as Romanticism. Romanticism declared that the only real foundation for a relationship was an intense bond of love. All practical considerations (heirs, status, property) were deemed either negligible or irrelevant. The Marriage of Reason gave way to the Marriage of Feeling. We were now left to choose our own partners, without reference to the wishes of anyone else, be it family or society. The ideal lover was to be found by Instinct, not by Reason.

The idea of following an 'Instinct' took on an enormous role in the story of love. Far from being a passing folly, the feeling of being 'in love' was now interpreted as a supremely reliable guide to half a century or more of conjugal happiness. The arrival of this feeling was understood to be a little mysterious: one couldn't predict it, justify it, or wish it to occur at will. It would simply descend upon us in the presence of certain people for reasons that lay outside conscious understanding. It had elements in common with a religious visitation. One would become aware of a variety of symptoms, amply described in literature and art: a quickened heartbeat, a sense of having alighted on 'The One', difficulty sleeping, an urge to speak (to almost everyone) about the beloved and a desire to listen to music and go into nature, together with The One.

Romanticism's faith in the power of instinctive attraction has been touching and at points exhilarating, but it has also proved enormously problematic. In comparison with the hopes we harbour of love, the way most of our lives turn out can appear extremely disappointing. When we take into account the statistics on marital unhappiness and divorce, we must conclude that raw instinct alone cannot be judged an especially reliable method of locating the right partner. Our belief in instinct has been no friend of our chances of happiness. We can't go back to the Marriage of Reason, but we may need to look for a future beyond the Relationship of Instinct. At The School of Life, we anticipate – and are trying to create tools for – what we call a Psychological Relationship: a union where the best insights of psychology are brought to bear on the complex business of finding and maintaining love.

II
Why We Fall in Love with Particular People

It is tempting to describe our instinctive attractions to particular people as simply *mysterious*. It feels, as we put it tellingly, 'Romantic' *not* to analyse our feelings, and merely to follow their dictates with awe and abandon.

However, our feelings are not the mysterious yet intelligent lodestars we might wish them to be. They are, for the most part, plainly misleading. A sense of being in love with someone is seldom a prelude to long-term contentment. If we intend to get better at relationships, we must attempt to examine the calls of Romantic love rationally. This isn't a question of abandoning instinct, but of improving upon it.

The most notable aspect of our instinct in love is its *particularity*. We aren't capable of falling in love with just anyone; we are powerfully led by our 'types'. We may reject many good candidates who, on paper, could sound perfect. We may not be able to explain much more about their inadequacies other than to say weakly that they didn't 'feel right'. Alternatively, we can be powerfully impelled towards other candidates, this time less clearly suitable, for reasons wholly beyond our conscious command. We are extremely, fascinatingly *choosy*.

Why, then, do we fall in love with particular people and not others? Why do we have the types we do? What guides our attractions? We can identify three components:

1
An instinct for completion

One of the most powerful forces within love is the Instinct for Completion. All of us are radically incomplete: we lack a range of *qualities* in our characters, psychological but also physical. We might be missing calm, creativity, practical know-how, wit, strength or sensitivity. It is as if, somewhere within us, we recognise this incompleteness and experience an attraction whenever we enter the orbit of someone who possesses a complementary quality. Through love, we seek to make good a defect and to complete ourselves.

As all of us have very different kinds of incompleteness, it stands to reason that we will find very different people attractive. Certain candidates will have qualities that leave us cold, because we have these in spades already: we may not need, for example, someone who is as calm as we are. Things would threaten to get dangerously quiet. We might need an injection of creativity and irreverence instead. Our tastes will be as varied as our deficiencies.

This mechanism of attraction in love is similar to the

mechanism of attraction we have around styles of architecture and design. When it comes to buildings and interiors, we also operate with an instinct for completion. The places we call 'beautiful' (like the people we call 'attractive') are often those that have qualities we want but don't yet have enough of. Consider these two very different buildings (right). We are most likely to be drawn to one or the other on the basis of a quality we don't feel we possess enough of in ourselves. People who feel a painful lack of exuberance, drama and extravagance, and are overwhelmed by drabness and sobriety might be drawn to Vienna's Peterskirche. Those who feel an anxious lack of calm, coherence and serenity, and have too much chaos, activity and intensity, might feel moved by the simplicity of the St. Moritz Church in Augsburg.

Peterskirche, Vienna, 1733

Baptism Chapel, St. Moritz Church, Augsburg, 2008–2013

2
The instinct for endorsement

There is a second instinct that drives us in love: the Instinct for Endorsement. We have many issues and feelings that we are lonely with, misunderstood for and that most people don't get or are uninterested in: perhaps we dislike certain people who are generally popular; maybe we are anxious about things that others are robust around; we might have sorrows that no one else seems to share, or we could have excitements and interests that carry no echo in others.

We might then be powerfully attracted to people who seem to understand the lonely aspects of us. We love them for their ability to endorse fragile, isolated, offbeat traits. They 'get' us, in contrast to the legions of the insensitive who cannot.

When we are finally with the ideal endorsing candidate, we feel engaged in a small conspiracy against the rest of the world. We don't have to explain very much about ourselves. They just *know*. They 'get' things *quickly*, without us having to speak. They *read our souls*, so we don't have to spell out their contents in the normal, arduous way. Our love is a dividend of gratitude for their magical ability to understand.

Perhaps we really like doing jigsaw puzzles – an interest that our more intellectual friends scoff at. Or we have a sexual quirk that we have never dared to share with past partners. Or we have sympathy for a political figure that everyone else seems to despise. Or we really love but also feel suffocated by our mother, and that has always sounded odd to people. Or no one seems to understand and forgive us for just how stressed we get around administrative tasks. Or we used to love crawling under our bed when we were a child – and we still like that part of us but we don't find it easy to bring it into the open. All of this the ideal partner will – on their own – simply *know*.

The way we approach love as adults is highly shaped by how we experienced love as children.

3
The instinct for familiarity

The way we approach love as adults is highly shaped by how we experienced love as children. In adulthood we will be attracted to people who remind us – more or less unconsciously – of the people we loved as children. The idea seems unnerving because of a natural feeling of disgust around thinking of parental figures as sexual. But this is not the point. It isn't that we are attracted to people who are in every way like our parents. It's just that, with unnerving symmetry, some of the qualities we find most attractive in adults are those that were once manifest in our caregivers from childhood. The affection of our partners can end up tinged with a feeling of familiarity. In their arms, in an emotional sense, we come home.

And, without anyone giving the matter too much thought, they sweetly call us 'baby'.

III

Our Problems with the People We Are Attracted To

Our society encourages us not to probe our three Instincts (for Completion, Endorsement and Familiarity) too much. We are encouraged to 'go with our feelings' and to 'trust our instincts'.

However, a degree of wisdom begins with the knowledge that our instincts will at points be extremely misleading. This is a feature of all human instinct, not merely the affectionate kind. We need only study our instinct for food: half of the rich world's population is obese and addicted to excess fat, sugar and salt. We're not spontaneous experts in knowing what is good for us.

An instinct is not easy to discount or dislodge, but it is possible to improve upon it and train it towards maturity. We will always be creatures of instinct, but we can learn to manage our drives more effectively. By doing so, we will radically improve our chances of finding someone we can love successfully over the long term.

1
The problem with our instinct for completion

The Instinct for Completion drives us towards strengths in others that promise to compensate for weaknesses in our own natures. What this means in practice is that, in order to become complete, two things must happen: we need to be willing to *learn* things and our partner must be willing to *teach* us things. And vice versa. The success of love will depend on success at *learning* and *teaching*.

Unfortunately, we tend to fail badly in both areas. We can decide that we don't really want to be taught. We don't want to change; change is painful. So although we're attracted to strengths in others, we don't necessarily accept that we have to correct the weaknesses in ourselves that fired our attractions in the first place. We are asking, in effect, to be educated by the other but we don't factor in that we might be reluctant pupils. Close up, we resist the lessons that we were, from afar, drawn to – and end up feeling patronised, humiliated and 'got at' by our partner.

Furthermore, our partner may not always be the tolerant, wise teacher we might have needed. However patient they might be in other contexts, they will be at risk of getting scared and offended by our flaws. They may become intemperate teachers from an overwhelming fear that they have married an idiot and ruined their lives. No wonder they may deliver their lessons sarcastically or with humiliating menace.

2
The problem with our
instinct for endorsement

The Romantic script of love tells us that a true lover will and must understand us *without us needing to speak*. They will endorse our lonely, confused, hard-to-reach aspects just by intuition.

This is very touching, but a huge problem in the long-term. It dissuades us from the difficult but necessary task of explaining ourselves: what we want, how we feel, why we are sad, what irritates us. We start to believe that a good lover should simply know the contents of our minds without us doing anything to share them. The fact that they understood *parts* of our minds so well, and so naturally, at one particular point leads to the counter-productive feeling that they should therefore understand the whole of our minds at all times – breeding a marked reluctance to explain (it doesn't feel very Romantic, we might say).

The background problem is that we are deeply complex creatures. Realistically, no human being will be able to feel their way intuitively into all areas of anyone else's mind. This means that in many situations that are very important to us, and in which we'd ideally like wordless understanding, we will not find rapid or easy endorsement from the person our instincts lead us to. In many cases, our unformulated needs will simply be met with deep, blank incomprehension or irritating error.

One of the great dangers of our Instinct for Endorsement is that it leads, when frustrated, to an outbreak of sulking. Sulking is a highly distinctive phenomenon within the psychology of love. Crucially, we don't sulk with just anyone. We reserve our sulks for people we believe should understand us but happen not to on a given occasion. We could explain what is wrong to them, of course, but if we did so, it would mean that they had failed to understand us intuitively and therefore that they were not worthy of love.

A sulk is one of the odder gifts of love. Our incensed background belief that a good lover should just know explains why on the evening when they unwittingly cause us offence at a party, we will sit quietly in the car on the way home and will reply with a simple 'Nothing' when they enquire if anything is up. When we get home, we'll disappear straight into the bathroom and bolt the door –

and when they ask again, 'Please tell me what is wrong', we'll remain silent with our arms folded, for we implicitly believe that a true lover – someone really worthy of our affection – would be able to read our intentions through the bathroom panel, through our outer casing and into the caverns of our burnt and pained souls.

3
The problem with our instinct for familiarity

a) The Repetition Dynamic

We are led by instinct to potential partners who feel familiar. In many ways, adult love is a search for a rediscovery of emotions first known in childhood. In order to prove attractive, the partner we pick must re-evoke many of the feelings we once had around parental figures.

However, parental figures may not merely be associated with tenderness and understanding; they may have mixed up their love with a host of problematic components. For example, they might have been depressed, unreliable, humiliating or chaotic. These qualities may now be the very things we need to find present in someone before we can experience ourselves as 'in love' with them. We may reject candidates without particular flaws and not even know why, simply saying that they are 'too nice' or 'a bit boring'. These are code terms for: 'unlikely to bring me the sort of problems that feel necessary in their familiarity'; or 'unable to make me suffer in the ways I need to in order to love'.

We might go so far as to say that we don't primarily want to be happy with the partner we choose. We want a partner to feel *familiar* – and this may mean that we are driven to seek out unhappy circumstances, if the affection we knew as children was connected with certain sorts of pain.

Following patterns laid down in childhood, we might say: I feel I'm in a close relationship when the other person bosses me about a lot, doesn't pay me much attention and tends to withhold affection, gets irritated by minor things I do or don't do, feels intellectually superior to me and lets me know it, or makes me feel furtive and ashamed about my body.

The Repetition Dynamic is what we call the odd tendency in relationships where we repeatedly go for partners with a very flawed nature who don't allow us to flourish or find happiness. This tendency is very hard to see in oneself but far easier to spot in others. It seems like a mistake, but it's far more intentional than this. At an unconscious level, we have no option but to follow a path of unhappy love laid down in childhood.

There is no blame here. Many people who cared for us had problematic aspects that they didn't choose. If they caused us trouble, it wasn't because they meant to. Still, we have to deal with the legacy.

b) *The Recoil Dynamic*

Challenging past experiences can also shape our relationship instincts in a very different way. Instead of being drawn to an adult who reminds us of a parent, our instincts may turn emphatically in the opposite direction. Something in our younger experience was so difficult that any sign of similarity between a parent and a prospective partner becomes deeply off-putting. We call this the Recoil Dynamic.

The reason why this can turn into a problem is that almost all parents have good as well as bad sides. When we suffer from the Recoil Dynamic, we may want to escape the bad but, along the way, can end up developing allergies to a lot of what was good. Maybe a parent was deeply creative, but had an appalling temper: now we can't stomach anyone creative. Maybe a parent was very clever, but humiliating: now we can't stomach anyone clever. Maybe a parent was good at business, but emotionally cold: now we can't stomach anyone who succeeds in commerce.

We may therefore have no internal option but to end up with people who are without qualities that would actually have benefited us, that would have nurtured us and with which we are by nature in sympathy. Our friends can find this puzzling. They may ask how someone so creative – and whose mother was too – could be with a partner like that. Or how someone from such an economically competent family could have ended up with this kind of layabout. In such circumstances, we should look for telltale evidence of the Recoil Dynamic.

Good quality in a difficult parent	Recoil requirement
High economic competence	Very unimpressive around money
Ordered and punctual	Freewheeling and chaotic
Socially poised and polite	Blunt and uncouth
Obviously intelligent	Very unintellectual

IV
Improving
Our Problematic
Instincts

1
Improving the instinct
for completion

We are not helpless before our instincts. By understanding
the way they work, we can take steps to attenuate their
worst consequences. We can learn to be intelligently
suspicious of our first impulses, and submit them to
reasoned examination before following their commands.

Not only do we need someone who possesses the qualities
we need; we also require something else that our instinct
fails to inform us about: a willingness in ourselves to hear
the lessons and take the steps that will help us become
the more rounded and balanced people we would like to
be. The fact that the other possesses the relevant aptitude
does not entail that we will be good at learning from them.
Having the weakness doesn't mean we'll automatically
be a willing and fast-learning pupil. We need to become
better students of what we want the other to teach us.

Our instinct aims at completion but massively fails to
register the difficulty of the process of being completed.
Instinct might take us to someone who in principle has
the strengths we're missing, but the relationship becomes

an agony when we grow offended by the idea of learning. We (understandably, but unfairly) feel we've got together with an oppressive tyrant who only notices our failings and is constantly on at us.

.

It's not that instinct is stupidly wrong in the direction it points us to; it's just that it is radically insufficient on its own. It is a good instinct, but, taken alone, it creates immense opportunities for relationship sorrows. A flourishing relationship should be a forum in which we teach each other many things and gracefully learn in turn. If we understand ourselves properly, we will know that there are many sides of us that need improvement. Love aims to be a safe arena in which two people can gently teach and learn how to grow into better versions of themselves. Teaching and learning does not symbolise an abandonment of love: it is the basis upon which we can develop into better lovers and, more broadly, better people.

If we understand ourselves properly, we will know that there are many sides of us that need improvement.

2
Improving the instinct
for endorsement

Our sulking and our belief in intuitive understanding has its touching side, evoking the enormous faith that we place in our partner's capacity to interpret us. But part of becoming an adult must be to believe that we cannot continue to expect others to read our minds if we have not previously laid out their contents through the (admittedly very cumbersome) medium of words. Even the most intelligent, sensitive lover cannot be expected to navigate around us without a lot of patiently articulated verbal indications of our desires and intentions.

Those charming early lucky guesses about what our lovers feel should not fool us for too long. Even in a very successful relationship, there is only a tiny amount that a lover should be expected to know of their beloved without it having been explained in language. We should not become furious when our lovers don't guess right. Rather than bolting our mouths and retreating into a sulk, we should have the courage to try to explain; to teach them calmly.

3
Improving the instinct
for familiarity

a) The Repetition Dynamic

The instinct for Familiarity leads us to two kinds of difficult types: people who have the same bad qualities as parental figures; and people who have none of the bad qualities as parental figures, but none of their good qualities either.

Two responses to these problems are often suggested by outsiders: that we should leave a troubling person, or that we should change our types. Both of these are very hard. At the School of Life, we are pessimistic about whether human beings can ever completely change the types of people they are attracted to.

Therefore, we offer a different solution: we believe that we should direct our efforts to changing the way we characteristically deal with the difficulties we are attracted to. At present, the way we tend to deal with the difficulties we are attracted to is in the manner of the children we once were. Our pattern of response is riddled with some of the problems that a young person might make. For example: we over-personalise issues that we are not principally responsible for; we don't explain our distress; we panic; we retreat into silence; we sulk.

In other words, there is an enormous opportunity to move from a child to an adult pattern of response in relation to the difficulties we are attracted to. What may be making our relationships awful is not simply that (for instance) we're attracted to someone who is a bit fiery, distant or manically busy, but that we continue to react to these issues as we did when, long ago in childhood, we first met with them. There is a properly grown-up – less agitated, less fragile – response that in principle we could have and that would make almost all the difference.

For most tricky characteristics to which we might instinctively be drawn, we can distinguish a child's reaction and an ideal adult response.

Our past may have assigned us an instinctive draw towards tricky people. But how we deal with them, once we're together, is open to revision. It makes all the difference whether we can move from column B to column C.

A: Tricky behaviour	B: Child reaction	C: Ideal adult reaction
Shouting	'It's all my fault...'	'It's something in them.'
Crushing intelligence	'I'm stupid.'	'That's interesting...'
Depressed	'I have to fix you.'	'I'll do my best, but I'm not ultimately responsible for your mindset...'
Frightening	'I deserve this.'	'I'm not intimidated by you.'
Distracted, preoccupied	Attention-seeking: 'Notice me'.	'You're busy; I'm busy, that's OK...'

b) The Recoil Dynamic

In the Recoil Dynamic, a pattern of behaviour has been experienced as so dangerous that one seeks its opposite as the natural escape. They were horrible and also scholarly, well organised, polite, creative or rich, so the latter attributes become toxic. We feel that everyone who doesn't have those attributes will be nice: we look for recoil qualities that are directly the opposite of the toxic qualities.

The trouble is that, with time, the recoil qualities tend to annoy us too. At first, it's a relief to be with someone who doesn't have the characteristics we've grown allergic to. Then we start to criticise our partners for the very qualities our instincts sought them out for. It's not surprising we do this, because we've been taught by experts (in childhood) how to put down these kinds of people.

Our difficult parent not only made their own merits toxic, they simultaneously taught us how to criticise those who lacked those merits. Our memories retain a clear education in how to attack the very thing we're drawn to in recoil. We are highly skilled at being crushing: we were taught by world experts from the earliest age!

A: Types we're drawn to	B: What we know well how to say
Non-intellectual	'You're a fucking idiot.'
Relaxed, disorganised	'Get your shit together.'
Socially modest	'You're vulgar.'
Shy	'You're so boring.'
Economically unimpressive	'You're so poor.'
Uncomplaining, unassertive	'You're a wimp.'

One suggestion is just to stop dating Recoil people. The advice is to transform our instincts (or dramatically override them) and learn to be attracted to people who have the good qualities of parental figures, but – by good fortune – not their problematic sides. But this is hard. A more realistic goal is to accept that we're probably always going to be drawn to Recoil qualities, but we can learn to manage them less aggressively and with a greater degree of forgiveness.

We could learn to feel rather differently about people who possess Recoil qualities, because the rebound qualities aren't bad in themselves.

Qualities of a difficult parent that became toxic	Recoil qualities we like	Critical things we say	Nicer things we could say
Highly intelligent	Non-intellectual	'You're a fucking idiot.'	'Many important things aren't complicated.'
Driven, very organised	Relaxed, a bit disorganised	'Get your shit together.'	'So what? You can be you.'
Socially modest, shy	Gregarious, socially ambitious	'You're a snob; you're pretentious.'	'You're confident and friendly and we don't have to do everything together.'
Powerful personality	Slightly shy	'You're so boring.'	'You are a calming presence in my life.'
Rich	Economically unimpressive	'You're so poor.'	'Money isn't everything.'
Strong-willed	Compliant	'You're a wimp.'	'You're sweet.'

We have trouble with our partners because we've learned to respond to their Recoil qualities in a punitive manner.

We have trouble with our partners not because they are so awful, but because we've learned to respond to their Recoil qualities in a punitive manner. There is another way of handling them. The first thing is to keep clearly in mind that our partner is doing us a favour: for example, the unintellectual person is sparing us the traumatic humiliation we would have around a scholarly type. The rather disorganised person is protecting us from the distress we would feel if we were with someone highly methodical and organised. We should keep reminding ourselves of the awkward truth that certain qualities are difficult for us. It's not a mistake that we've been drawn to this person. We should remind ourselves that our room for manoeuvre is limited. The task is not to hate a partner for their deficiencies; it is to get interested, in a kindly way, in their development.

V

Obstacles to Finding Love

1
The challenge of reciprocation

Ostensibly, we all want love – but when love actually starts to be reciprocated, it may prove intensely alarming. We can start to think very badly of the person we liked only a little time before. We typically accuse the now-reciprocating lover of two things.

We feel they are naive in finding us wonderful. They like us only because they don't know how to read human nature. They are gullible and too easily taken in by people. It's hard to respect seducers who are so psychologically unastute. They are too intellectually limited to 'read' us properly. They don't perceive the less appealing, more disturbed, darker aspects of who we are. Their affections therefore seem precarious and dangerous: they would surely cool if they discovered the truth about us, which is frightening. Therefore, we take extra care to give little away. We feel lonely because, despite the love, big parts of us aren't in any position to be acknowledged.

Also, we accuse these partners of being 'needy'. They start to rely on us and want us a lot – and, in the process, appear weak and not quite grown up. We wonder why they can't stand on their own two feet, like a normal adult.

We're accusing the lover of being in the wrong. But really, the problem almost certainly lies with us. We should consider what is causing us to resort to the words 'naive' and 'needy'. Their alleged naivety is our doing. They think us wonderful, but only because this is the way we have presented ourselves. We have been extraordinarily successful at hiding all our shadow sides from them. It is not they who are naive, it's we who are good liars. It is normal, during seduction, to throw the light on the more positive aspects of our characters, but there is a phenomenon that goes beyond this, an extreme seduction, where we assiduously hide everything problematic in our characters. What lies behind extreme seduction is self-hatred. We think that, at heart, we are unacceptable people, that no one could really love us if they saw our true selves, and therefore we develop great skill at camouflaging ourselves. This works, at a price of devastating loneliness.

The solution isn't to blame the other person for naivety; it is to learn to show others who we truly are, on the basis of loosening our suspicion of ourselves. We need to make the initially implausible leap of faith that we might be acceptable to someone else who knew us more completely; we don't necessarily have to lie in order to deserve love. Furthermore, perhaps the lover isn't naive at all. They can see us for what we are: they have noticed the nervous efforts at seduction, the manic attempts to please, the shame about our true nature. And they don't mind; they know we're not quite who we say we are, but they know we're not so bad either – and the reality is, they aren't wrong. So it's not that they are naive about us, but that we're naive about them; they're not the simpletons we judged them to be. They know human nature. They know that, of course, everyone has shadow sides. They've made their peace with theirs. They would like us to make peace with ours. Ahead of us, they understand that both they and we are worthy of love. We give up on extreme seduction and learn the art of intelligent self-revelation: the art of gradually and honestly unfolding our complex humanity to a generous witness.

As for 'neediness', the term can all too quickly summon up an image of disreputable figures with a lack of boundaries and an insatiable, unwarranted appetite for our time. Perhaps they call us three times an hour to 'check in' or get nervous if we go into the next room. There are, of

Showing
need is a
precondition
of strength
rather than
weakness.

course, a few pathologically dependent people at large, but a lot of the time – far more than is generally accepted – the person who has the problem isn't the 'needy' person, it is us: the ones who are doing the accusing.

We will feel that someone is sickeningly 'needy' when we don't see ourselves as appropriate targets of someone else's need. Somewhere inside, we don't trust that we are reliable, strong, dependable, admirable or decent; we aren't quite grown-up – and so those who need something from us therefore come across as deranged and fitting targets for mockery. At the first sign that someone is becoming reliant on us, we flinch. We suspect that someone who needs us enough to depend on us for a pleasant weekend or a Tuesday evening must be diseased.

However, the solution isn't necessarily to try to change the lover by telling them to stop asking so much. They most probably aren't asking too much at all; they are just strong enough to reveal that they aren't invulnerable. Showing need is a precondition of strength rather than weakness. We should revise our view of ourselves, to see ourselves as more or less plausible people for someone else to stand in need of. The fear of 'needy' people is only a species of self-hatred rippling outwards to tar our lover.

A reduction of self-hatred does not depend on self-boosterism (telling ourselves how great we are). We should learn to tolerate ourselves, not by believing we are wonderful, but via a secure realisation that everyone is both OK and sometimes a bit awful. We can be cured of our uncommonly vicious self-suspicion by a more accurate vision of what constitutes normality. Of course we are a bit weak, a bit sly and a bit foolish, to put it gently. But so is everyone. We are no more idiotic or wayward than the next person. We can embrace a person's hopes for a close and deep relationship with us simply on the basis that we are all a bit odd and broken. The need that the lover has of us is not delusional; it is an accurate request that any flawed human might make of another comparably damaged example.

To cope better with the challenges of reciprocated love, we need to nuance what we believe love means. We are appalled by reciprocated love when we operate with a background idea of sentimental love. This states that loving ourselves is what we can do *only* when we are totally pure, and that loving another is what we can do *only* when someone is perfect. Yet we are, of course, all deeply flawed.

The origins of a sentimental interpretation of love usually lie with parents who could not tolerate their children's shadow sides. Somewhere in the past, a child had to be perfect in order to deserve affection. Tantrums, bad habits and nasty thoughts had to be banished. The child became outwardly 'good' and inwardly ashamed and lonely. We need to move towards a more humane and mature model of complex love; a love that tolerates imperfection and ambivalence, that accepts that we can have faults *and* love ourselves and can see the faults of another person *and* still love them.

2
The fear of happiness

It is normal to expect that we will always – almost by nature – actively seek out our own happiness in love.

It is therefore odd and a little unnerving to find how we can in love sometimes act as if we were deliberately trying to ruin our chances of getting what we wanted. When going on dates with candidates we are keen on, we may suddenly lapse into unnecessarily opinionated and antagonistic behaviour. Or when we are in a relationship with someone we love, we may drive them to distraction through repeated unwarranted accusations and angry explosions – as if we were somehow willing to bring on the sad day when, exhausted and frustrated, the beloved would be forced to walk away, still sympathetic but unable to take our elevated degree of suspicion and drama.

Such behaviour can't be put down to mere bad luck. It deserves a stronger, more intentional term: self-sabotage. We are familiar enough with the fear of failure, but it appears that success can bring about as many anxieties, which may culminate in a desire to scupper our chances of happy love in a bid to restore our peace of mind.

There is a basic truth at the heart of this worry: when we love someone, we risk loss. They could turn against us, succumb to a rare illness, or turn their attentions elsewhere. There is no way these possibilities can ever be entirely eliminated. What is distinctive about the self-saboteur is not that they are aware of the possibilities of loss, but that these possibilities affect them so acutely.

As ever, an explanation has to start with childhood. The self-saboteur is one who has grown to find the price of hope too high to pay. We may, when we were younger, have been exposed to brutal disappointments at a time when we were too fragile to withstand them. Perhaps we hoped our parents would stay together and they didn't. Or we hoped our father would eventually come back from another country and he stayed there. Perhaps we dared to love an adult and, after a period of happiness, they swiftly and oddly changed their attitude and let us down. Somewhere in our characters, a deep association has been forged between hope and danger, along with a corresponding preference to live quietly with disappointment, rather than more freely with hope.

The solution is to remind ourselves that we can, despite our fears, survive the loss of hope. We are no longer those who suffered the disappointments responsible for our present timidity. The conditions that forged our caution are no longer those of adult reality. The unconscious mind may, as is its wont, be reading the present through the lenses of decades ago, but what we fear will happen has, in truth, already happened; we are projecting into the future a catastrophe that belongs to a past we have not had the chance to fathom or mourn adequately. We are suffering from a localised immaturity: an archaic part of us remains as it was when we were a child. It has not been able to grow and shed its terrors. The intensity of the fear is based on the idea that we can only bring childhood resources to the problem. We still feel the same age as we were when we met a horrendous loss.

But, in fact we're big now. We have the capacity to cope very well. Should this relationship fail, we'll be sad for a while but won't actually be destroyed. We are not in as much danger as the primitive part of the mind thinks – and as we once were. We are no longer the children for whom loss was unbearable.

3
Fixation

One of the key things that can go wrong in our search for love is that we get fixated on a particular person who turns out not to be a promising or realistic option. It may be that the person is in another country, with someone else, definitely not interested in us – or even dead.

Fixation is the conviction that there is only one person we can genuinely love, even if we can't actually have a relationship with them. When a new person comes along who might potentially be a good partner for us, we reject them. We feel it would be disloyal to the individual we are fixated upon, even though they may neither know nor care about this.

Fixation disguises itself as a very Romantic attitude. Our love is unrequited, impossible – yet also seems especially intense and pure. The most famous love story of the 18th century, Goethe's *The Sorrows of Young Werther*, is about a fixation in love. Werther falls passionately in love with Charlotte, who likes him but doesn't love him back – and soon gets married to someone else. There are plenty of other nice women around who are single, attractive and interested in Werther. But Werther has no time for them. The only one he cares for is Charlotte, the one who can't care for him.

This sounds Romantic, but to loosen ourselves from the grip of our fixations, we should realise that a devotion to an unrequited situation is in essence a clever way of ensuring we won't end up in a relationship at all. Fixation is really a fear of love.

The fear may be motivated by a dread of possible loss, self-hatred or a fear of self-revelation: a reluctance to let anyone into the secret parts of ourselves. These are the issues we have to grapple with, rather than the surface matters we endlessly discuss (how to persuade the uninterested lover to love us; and how, despite their rejection, they are so perfect).

Once we see fixation for what it really is, the idea that a particular person could be so important stops looking like a great act of love and devotion. Fixation is not a manifestation of love; it is a calculated commitment to an obstacle to finding love.

Another move to unfixate ourselves is not to tell ourselves that we don't like this person or to attempt to forget how much we are attracted to them. It is to get very serious and specific about what the attraction is based on, and then to realise that the qualities we admire exist in other people who don't have the problems that are currently making a fulfilling relationship impossible. The careful investigation of what we love about one person shows us – paradoxically but liberatingly – that we could also love someone else.

Understanding what we like in a person – what gives us pleasure – is therefore a central anti-fixation move. By strengthening our attachment to qualities, we are weakening our attachment to specific individuals. When we properly grasp what draws us to one lover, we necessarily identify qualities that are available in other lovers too. What we really love isn't this specific creature, but a range of qualities we located in them first, normally because they were the most conspicuous examples of a repository for them. This is where the problem started, because over-conspicuous people tend to attract too much attention, get over-subscribed and are then in a position to offer only very modest reciprocation.

Yet in reality, the qualities can't exist only there. They are necessarily generic and will be available under other, less obvious, guises – once we know how to look. This is not an exercise in getting us to give up on what we really want. The liberating move is to see that what we want exists in places beyond the pain-inducing characters we have already identified it in.

4
The inability to
leave someone

For many of us, a major obstacle to getting into a good relationship is an inability to leave an unfulfilling one to which we are deeply but unhappily committed. Although we may long to flee, we don't feel ruthless enough to break away. Our present lover seems so content with us; they have emitted so many signals of their trust and investment in our future; they are so vulnerable in front of us, that we can't bring ourselves to be the bearers of terrible news. We fear two things above all: that they will collapse without us and never find happiness again, and that our rejection will render them immensely furious and vengeful. We are at once concerned and scared.

Almost always, our fears are unrealistic. People leave each other all the time, almost always without anything properly horrible happening. What is striking, then, is why some of us can be so afraid of upsetting someone, projecting onto another a degree of extreme fragility that they are unlikely to have. Of course they will be furious and upset for a while, but they will, most likely, survive.

It is not so much the idea that they won't be able to cope that holds us back; it's the feeling that we won't be able to cope with upsetting them. We have become people for whom the thought of upsetting another person (even for very good reasons) has become intensely troubling.

As ever, we can look to childhood for answers. We are likely to have experienced moments when adults around us seemed unable to take bad news, be it from us or from others in their lives. They slammed doors, screamed, threatened to kill themselves, threw things at us…. There was no room for us to bring our problems to the table. The parents seemed agitated and unhappy enough as it was. 'Do you want to kill me or something?' a parent might have shouted, the day we got caught stealing a ball or had a nosebleed over the carpet. We took care never to do that, or anything else like it, again. Perhaps the reality was not as bad as it seemed to a five-year-old child, but that is the point: children are unable to sense the difference between catastrophe and an evening of deep but passing upset in an easily agitated adult. The two merge into one another and create a confusion – which can survive deep into adulthood – between unhappiness and suicidal grief. A traumatic encounter with fragility may leave us feeling that we must never, at any cost, be the bearers of terrible news. We strive to be people-pleasers. However, in the realm of love, politeness about the future ruins lives.

The truth is that our lingering childhood fears are likely to be phantasms. Certainly there will be some momentary drama. The news will be very shocking. There will be tears. There could be screaming. Something might be thrown and broken. But humans can survive a night of hysterical crying. It won't be the end of the story. The novel of the rejected partner's life, which on the night of the break-up will look as if it had ground to an appalling end amid damp tissues and vows never ever to love again, will of course carry on. The sun will rise again. The next chapter might read something like this: *'After Nabil told her it was over, Mel cried for a month. She could barely get out of bed. She ate almost nothing. She told friends that her life was over and that she would never, ever get through this. Once she called up Nabil to beg him to come back. He was very accommodating and embarrassed – but didn't. Then, as spring came around, work got busier and Mel started to feel better. A few weeks into April, she had a drink with Nick, a friend of a colleague at work. He was lovely and invited her to the cinema the following weekend....'*

We are inclined to forget, too, that there are many forms of harm. We don't only harm by being brutal with others;

we can as easily – and perhaps more deeply – harm someone by seeming very nice to them, while wasting their years in a union to which we know all along we don't feel committed. Part of properly growing up is knowing the difference between seeming nice and being nice – the latter requiring one to do things to a lover that will for a time enrage and devastate them. For real kindness, we need to have the courage to allow ourselves to be hated. The psychological imperative to appear nice at all costs will guarantee that we'll be nothing other than quietly, exceptionally cruel. We owe it to those we no longer love to kill all hope and allow them to hate us, confident that we can withstand their anger. In the end, that is true kindness.

5
A lack of confidence
in seduction

The need to seduce prospective lovers into our beds and lives is fraught with the dangers of humiliation. But how afraid we are of humiliation depends on one thing in particular: how attached we are to our own dignity.

There's a kind of under-confidence that can afflict us in seduction when we grow too keen never to appear ridiculous. It is impossible to seduce someone and not run a serious risk of looking absurd: they may have a partner already; they may think we're repulsive; they may not show up at the restaurant; they might say 'Don't be so silly!' when we touch their hand. If we are desperate never to look foolish, we can't dare to do very much and thereby, from time to time, miss out on the best opportunities of our lives.

At the heart of our under-confidence in seduction is a skewed picture of how dignified a normal person can be. We imagine that it might be possible, after a certain age, to place ourselves beyond mockery. We trust that it is an option to lead a good love life without regularly making a complete idiot of ourselves. It isn't.

The way to greater confidence isn't to reassure ourselves of our own dignity; it's to grow at peace with the inevitable nature of our ridiculousness. We are idiots now, we have been idiots in the past, and we will be idiots again in the future – and that is OK. There aren't any other options available for human beings.

Once we learn to see ourselves as already, and by nature, foolish, it doesn't matter so much if we do one more thing that might look quite stupid. The person we try to kiss could indeed think us ridiculous. But if they did so, it wouldn't be news to us; they would only be confirming what we had already gracefully accepted long ago: that we, like them – and every other person on the earth – are a nitwit. The risk of trying and failing would have its sting substantially removed. The fear of humiliation would no longer stalk us in the shadows of our minds. We would grow free to give things a go by accepting that failure was the norm. And every so often, amid the endless rebuffs we'd have factored in from the outset, it would work: we'd get a kiss, we'd make a friend, we'd get married... .

It's important to recall another point to give us confidence: if we did kiss, make a friend, and marry, we'd almost certainly be quite unhappy with this partner a lot of the time. Our intimidated feelings before a prospective lover stem from a melodramatic sense of how much is at stake. We hesitate to ask for a number or go out for dinner because we feel we are in the presence of an exalted being who appears to have no ordinary frailties and potentially holds the keys to earthly satisfaction in their hands. No wonder we may be too shy to speak or stumble over our words when we do so. The wiser response is to remember that this paragon of apparent beauty and perfection will, with time, prove to be much more complicated than they appear and will at points be heart-wrenchingly disappointing and maddening. This dark knowledge should relax us as we struggle to speak to them: we are not, in fact, faced with a divine being balancing our fate in their well-formed hands. They are an ordinary creature beset with all the tensions, compromises and blind spots we know from our own selves. We can approach our date with the down-to-earth confidence of one misery-inducing human reaching out to another to start a relationship that will, in time, at many points, feel like an enormous mistake. We can import into the seduction phase some of the (usefully relaxing) ingratitude that we naturally experience once a relationship has started – and use it to get love going.

The road to greater confidence in seduction begins with a ritual of telling oneself solemnly every morning, before heading out for the day, that one is a muttonhead, a cretin, a dumbbell and an imbecile, rarely capable of being happy for longer than fifteen minutes. One or two more acts of folly should, thereafter, not matter very much.

6
Impatience

One of the most important principles for choosing a lover sensibly is not to feel in any hurry to make a choice. Being satisfied with being single is a precondition of satisfactory coupledom. We cannot choose wisely when remaining single feels unbearable. We have to be at peace with the prospect of many years of solitude in order to have any chance of forming a good relationship, or we'll love no longer being single rather more than we love the partner who spared us being so.

Unfortunately, after a certain age, society makes singlehood feel dangerously unpleasant. Communal life starts to wither. People in couples are too threatened by the independence of the single to invite them around very often – in case they are reminded of something they might miss. Friendship and sex are, despite all the gadgets, remarkably hard to come by. No wonder then, that when someone even slightly decent comes along we cling to them, to our eventual enormous cost.

When sex was only available within marriage, people recognised that this led people to marry for the wrong

We should strive to make ourselves as much at peace as we can be with the idea of being alone.

reasons: to obtain something that was artificially restricted in society as a whole. Sexual liberation was intended to allow people to have a clearer head when choosing who they really wanted to be with. But the process remains half-finished. Only when we make sure that being single can be potentially as secure, warm and fulfilling as being in a couple will we know that people are choosing to pair up for the right reasons. It is time to liberate 'companionship' from the shackles of coupledom, and make it as widely and as easily available as sexual liberators wanted sex to be.

In the meantime, we should strive to make ourselves as much at peace as we can be with the idea of being alone for a long time. Only then do we stand a chance of deciding to be with someone on the basis of their own merits.

VI
Conclusion:
Realism

1
Difficulty and imagination

We often tell ourselves that we keep meeting no one with whom we could possibly go out. Even if we live in a city of millions and have access to billions more on our devices, we are clear about our situation: *there is no one out there for us.*

We here allege a different thesis. There are plenty of people out there for us, and we have already encountered a range of candidates it would be entirely plausible for us to be with; it's just that we are unable to see the opportunities. More particularly, we believe – rather wrongly – that there is no one out there 'good enough' for us. We feel we could do better, and yet – tellingly – we never do. To shake us from our proud and unhelpful assumption, there are two moves we can make.

Firstly, we should take an honest look at ourselves and wonder whether we really are such deserving, special beings. Our sense of how much of a prize we are often depends on a sense of our pleasing looks or our high status. Here, indeed, we may have a lot to be proud of. But a more fruitful kind of humility – and therefore gratitude and generosity towards our dates – might emerge from considering our personalities. Here there tends to be a veil of silence around our difficult sides. It is in few people's interests to inform us of quite what tricky types we are. Our parents are too kind, our friends lack an incentive, and our ex-lovers are more likely to have left us with a blithe claim that they needed more 'space' or were going to India, rather than explaining how nightmarish we could be. We therefore sally forth with a confident sense of our power to contribute a lot to any relationship and expect to receive ample gratitude from others just for looking their way. We can't tell that we are, in many ways, real trouble to be with.

We might be a proper pain in a range of ways: we don't like doing things differently; we don't like having to back down when we've decided on something; we don't listen very well to what the other person is saying; we struggle to share responsibility; we are demanding, but not good at explaining why certain things are so important to us; we work too much, we have a tendency to scold rather than gently teach; we get worked up about things that other people don't care about (but don't seem to notice their boredom).

Excessive self-hatred is a great enemy of relationships,

but so too is excessive self-love. Only by realising that we're not perfect in certain hard-to-see areas can we be liberated to get together with people who are not perfect either; the only kind of people we are ever going to meet.

Realism about oneself leads to a more realistic engagement with others. It helps us compromise constructively around our ideas of who might be good enough for us. Of course, we have got a lot of merits, but we need to compromise because we're difficult people to be with. We will be a challenge for anyone.

A broadening of options emerges not only from realising our flaws; it also comes from taking a second, more imaginative, look at the litany of flawed potential partners whom we have grown used to dismissing so quickly and ruthlessly. We need to rediscover the role of the imagination in the genesis of love. When our imaginations are switched off, we judge people on the very obvious things about them. We meet someone who is quite nice, but their nose is big. That's a no. Or they are an engineer, and engineers are unsophisticated. So that's a no. Maybe they are rich, and rich people are snobs. A no too. Perhaps their hair is thinning and bald people aren't our thing. No. Or their wrists are knobbly; no. When we're in an unimaginative mode, we strike many people off the list of possibles very quickly. In this frame of mind, we have a relatively brief tick-list of things that interest (or repel) us. We feel it only takes a moment or two to sum someone up – and fire them.

But what we call imagination means sensitivity to the less obvious things. One scans past the surface and wonders about what else might be going on in a person. They look conventional and a bit formal, but they could turn out to have playful and wild sides too. They look mousey, but maybe they are also very witty around people they know well. They do have a slightly wonky nose, but their eyes are very tender and their lips surprisingly sensual. They have a job that sounds unimpressive, but their interests are very broad and they might be the ideal person to go round an antiques market with. With the help of imagination, we start to engage with quieter virtues that we can't see if we look head on. Practising imagination is a key to love. In a way it is love, for we all ultimately have to be considered imaginatively in order to be tolerated and forgiven over the long term. By thinking imaginatively, we're not being disloyal to the true ambition of love; we're stumbling on the essence of what love involves.

2
'Good enough' and
obviously terrible

One of the factors that holds us back from committing to a partner is a feeling that it isn't normal for there to be certain areas of problem and compromise. We reject a situation from a background impression that, on the whole, love is said (especially in art) to be far better than this. Our ideals crush the available realities. But maybe what we're encountering isn't a bad relationship, just a normal one.

In the mid-20th century, the English psychoanalyst Donald Winnicott coined a phrase to help anxious parents doing their best but constantly worried that they were falling short of being perfect parents. The real goal, Winnicott said, wasn't to be ideal in every way, just to be 'good enough'. A child doesn't need a perfect parent. They need an ordinary, somewhat flawed, well-intentioned parent who will makes mistakes, have regrets, worry, get cross, then apologise; someone who will have other demands in their life that will sometimes have to take precedence, but who will still love and be kind and fulfil many of their needs. They will be 'good enough'. Winnicott was reassuring parents tortured by an unattainable ideal: people who judged their lives and themselves harshly by standards they could never reach. Ironically, these types risked being less warm and natural parents because they were constantly anxious about not being perfect. Human relationships, Winnicott was saying, can look quite bad and yet we're actually doing OK, considering the norm. This is a useful attitude to bring to our loves, for they too are unlikely to be perfect. But they are likely to be, in their way (and far more than we sometimes allow), acceptably 'good enough.'

There's a darker version of this move from the early 19th-century Danish philosopher Søren Kierkegaard. Kierkegaard was especially interested in the enormous choices humans constantly have to make and the paralysis that can ensue. We have to decide to get together with someone, possibly for the next fifty years. How to take on such a burden? How can we ever decide and move forward? In Kierkegaard's eyes, we can get stuck choosing because of one reason: we are so hopeful that we can choose well. We are convinced that there is one potentially very right choice and lots of very bad ones. That is why we are so careful, so choosy and so worried. Actually, Kierkegaard insists, we exaggerate the difference. We don't face a perilous moment of decision between an excellent path and a dark one, because everything we choose is going to be fairly grim in certain ways, because life is necessarily rather than incidentally awful. We are only ever faced with bad options – which is at once tragic and beautifully liberating. We don't need to be so fastidious about the business of choosing. Hence Kierkegaard's playfully, bleakly exasperated outburst from his book *Either/Or:*

> 'Marry, and you will regret it; don't marry, you will also regret it; marry or don't marry, you will regret it either way. Laugh at the world's foolishness, you will regret it; weep over it, you will regret that too; laugh at the world's foolishness or weep over it, you will regret both. Believe a woman, you will regret it; believe her not, you will also regret it…. Hang yourself, you will regret it; do not hang yourself, and you will regret that too; hang yourself or don't hang yourself, you'll regret it either way; whether you hang yourself or do not hang yourself, you will regret both. This, gentlemen, is the essence of all philosophy.'

In other words, whatever we choose will be a bit wrong, so we shouldn't agonise too much about any one choice we make. The real skill is not always to strive to make better choices; it's to know how to make our peace with our necessarily bad choices. We keep on supposing that our lives would turn out well if only we could somehow make an ideal right decision. But Kierkegaard is firmly opposed to this naive error. We should with cheer accept that we never had ideal options in the first place. This is not a curse on us: the same difficult truth has to be faced by everyone.

Both Winnicott and Kierkegaard are saying that there will always be something wrong around relationships. It sounds as if this might be a depressing message, but its effect is the reverse. If things are a bit bad, it's probably because we're doing it right. These thinkers are backing us away from an unhelpful ideal. They are inviting us to be more modest in our expectations of relationships, not to make us unhappy, but in order to help us make our peace with the only thing that is actually on offer: a radically imperfect but genuine love for another flawed person and a necessarily troubled but still valuable shared life beside them.

Credits

The School of Life is a global organisation helping people lead more fulfilled lives. It is a resource for helping us understand ourselves, for improving our relationships, our careers and our social lives – as well as for helping us find calm and get more out of our leisure hours. We do this through films, workshops, books, gifts and community. You can find us online, in stores and in welcoming spaces around the globe.